Amazing Women Athletes

☆ THE WOMEN'S HALL OF FAME SERIES ☆

Amazing Women Athletes

by
JILL BRYANT

Second
Story
Press

NATIONAL LIBRARY OF CANADA CATALOGUING IN PUBLICATION DATA

Bryant, Jill
Amazing women athletes

(The women's hall of fame series)
Includes bibliographical references.
ISBN 1-896764-44-4

1. Women athletes--Biography--Juvenile literature. I. Title.
II. Series: Women's hall of fame series.

GV697.A1B79 2001   j796'.092'2   C2001-902331-6

Edited by Ruth Chernia
Cover design by Stephanie Martin
Text design by Laura McCurdy
Photo edit by Vivian Harrower and Alexia Loumankis

Printed and bound in Canada

*Second Story Press gratefully acknowledges the support of the Ontario
Arts Council and the Canada Council for the Arts for our publishing
program. We acknowledge the financial support of the Government of
Canada through the Book Publishing Industry Development Program.*

Published by
SECOND STORY PRESS
720 Bathurst Street, Suite 301
Toronto, ON
M5S 2R4
www.secondstorypress.on.ca

For Zoë

✩ Table of Contents ✩

✿ Introduction ✿
Winning Women

WHAT IS IT that pushes professional athletes to train hard, to beat their personal records and to compete to the very best of their abilities? A dream. A dream to achieve something great. A dream to be the best. A dream to win. This book, which takes a close look at ten amazing women in international sports, reveals many dreams. Many of these have already come true. Other athletes are still competing, trying for gold, aiming to break a personal record or striving to perform more splendidly than ever before. Big dreams help push them to achieve.

This collection covers a variety of sports and features awe-inspiring athletes from North America and around the world. The women featured in this book are not always the most well-known or highest achieving athletes, though some are certainly famous. They are women who have not only accomplished tremendous athletic feats, but also have managed to overcome challenges that stood in the way of their goals. Some women faced prejudice, injuries or poor health; some had financial troubles; others didn't have much support from their home countries.

Many of the women in this collection have become excellent public speakers. They work to promote women in athletics and women who pursue male-dominated sports, such as hockey and jockeying. Others have used the fame they have achieved through sports to speak out on political issues that are important to them or to help charities with fundraising campaigns.

Like all successful athletes, these women truly love their sports. They are also fiercely competitive, with a keen desire to win. Another side of their personalities emerges in the way they interact with the public, the way they live their lives and the way they give so generously of themselves. The selfless nature demonstrated by these determined, strong-willed athletes is worthy of attention. This is perhaps the most admirable quality that these ten winning women possess. It makes them stand out.

Looking at the achievements of Annie Smith Peck and Bobbie Rosenfeld, who were active long ago when what women could do was more restricted than today, we can appreciate the struggles these women overcame. The opportunities for women in sports have improved tremendously over the past century, especially in the last four decades, partly because of the efforts of these groundbreaking pioneers. Today's women athletes face other challenges. Cathy Freeman fights to promote Aboriginal rights in Australia. Chantal Petitclerc, who races in a wheelchair, hopes to see her sport designated as a full-fledged Olympic event. Hayley Wickenheiser wants to see women hockey players participate in the professional leagues with men. She thinks this will happen someday soon.

This book celebrates the contributions of ten amazing women athletes from different countries and different times. Some have been dead for decades, some are retired; others are still competing and will be in the spotlight for several more years. You will find inspiration and gain confidence from the lives of these courageous and determined women.

1

Annie Smith Peck

1850 **1935**

HAVE YOU EVER dreamed of climbing a mountain? Annie Smith Peck sure did. She knew she would do it one day and the ambition wouldn't go away until she had mastered the sport. She was fearless and determined, and would go on to reach new heights for women in North America, South America and Europe.

Annie was an intelligent and ambitious woman who refused to let Victorian society tell her what women could and couldn't do. (Queen Victoria ruled England from 1837 to 1901. During this time women were expected to be "lady-like," prim and proper.) After completing grade school and

normal school (a school for training teachers), Annie wanted to attend university as her older brothers had done. Her
father couldn't believe his ears. Attend university? What
was his daughter thinking? In the 1870s young women did
not do such things!

Her father threatened to cut off Annie from her inheri-
tance, but she persisted. She said it would be unfair not to
support her decision when he had encouraged her brothers
to attend university. Finally, her father agreed. Annie was
thrilled! She enrolled in Classics at Ann Arbor University in
Michigan, and was awarded a Bachelor of Arts in 1878 at
the age of twenty-eight.

Annie taught for two years and then in 1881 completed
her Master of Arts. She took a position as professor of Latin
at Purdue University in Lafayette, Indiana. During a lecture,
Professor Jordan, the president of Stanford University,
talked about climbing a mountain in the Swiss Alps called
the Matterhorn. He said that few men could achieve such an
ambitious climb — and certainly no women! Annie raised
her eyebrows at this comment, but said nothing. She never
forgot this remark and decided that she would have a look
at this mountain someday to see if what he said was true.

When Annie was thirty-four years old, she left for
Europe. She planned to study in Germany, but also traveled
to Austria, Switzerland, Italy and France. Of course, she
made a point of visiting the famous Matterhorn in the Alps.
She considered trying a climb — and really wanted to — but
the timing wasn't good and she went back to her studies in
Germany. Annie knew she would return to the Matterhorn.
In the meantime, after a year in Germany, this accomplished scholar became the first female student to study at
the School of Classical Archaeology in Athens, Greece.

Then Annie returned to the United States and taught

Latin at Smith College in Northampton, Massachusetts. Annie enjoyed this appointment very much but, when she was denied a promotion to Head of the Department, her positive feelings about her job were crushed. Why wasn't she promoted? She knew it was simply because she was a woman. The unfairness of this enraged Annie so much that she quit and became a traveling lecturer. Her real plan was to devote more time to her dream: a career as a traveler and explorer.

She visited the west coast of the United States with her brother George Peck Junior, and climbed up to Cloud's Rest, the highest point in the Yosemite Mountains. Annie was the first woman to have reached the top, and she discovered that she loved mountain climbing! Every summer Annie practiced in the Adirondack and White Mountains of New Hampshire, which were near her

home. She had an idea that she might be able to publish articles about climbing in magazines. This would help her raise money for her own expeditions. Annie decided to climb a challenging mountain to make herself well-known. She planned to travel to South America, where there are mountains higher than any in North America.

But first Annie had unfinished business in Europe: the Matterhorn. How could she make this dream happen? Annie had to find enough money to support her trip because she was not a wealthy woman. She approached the owners of *Century Magazine* who agreed to give her money in exchange for articles about her trip and the climb. Annie climbed several mountains in Europe before attempting the Matterhorn. Defying the conventions of the times, she unfastened her heavy skirts and climbed in her knickers (loose-fitting, short pants women wore under their skirts)! She reached the summit at 14,703 feet (4524 meters) above sea level. This was a record for an American woman climber. Her climb brought her the celebrity she had hoped for. It also brought her much attention for shedding her skirts!

After conquering the Matterhorn, Annie climbed two mountains in Mexico. One of them, Mount Orizaba, is 18,660 feet (5742 meters) high. Annie was the first woman to reach such a height. Next she wanted to climb Mount Sorata in Bolivia. Unfortunately conflicts arose between the guide and the porters, who carry equipment and baggage. This caused many problems for the expedition, and Annie eventually had to give up when the porters refused to climb further.

Because giving up was not in Annie's nature, she had a difficult time dealing with this when she returned to the United States. She knew she had to try again. But how? She needed good porters, and she also needed money for the expedition. Finally she secured funding through two newspapers and several generous donors. She planned to hire local people as guides and porters on the climb. Then she met Victor Sintich, a European with lots of climbing experience, whom she hired to join her.

Annie was fifty-four years old when she began her second attempt at climbing Mount Sorata. Again, due to the harsh weather conditions, her companions refused to go beyond a certain height and Annie had to turn back. Then she decided to try a different mountain, Mount Huascarán in Peru, which was estimated to be about 25,000 feet (7692 meters) in height. She hired one man to accompany her and they took horses instead of porters to carry their food and climbing gear. They battled through snowstorms and avalanches during this climb and made it to 19,000 feet (5846 meters). But the weather conditions were awful and they could not continue.

Barely taking time to rest after this strenuous climb, Annie was keen to try again five days later. Unfortunately, terrible weather prevented Annie from getting as high as the previous attempt.

Feeling defeated, Annie was at a low point in her life. She returned to New York where she tried to write and lecture, but all she really wanted to do was climb. She was very poor. In 1906, she gathered enough money for her third and fourth attempts at Mount Huascarán. Neither was successful, but before returning home, Annie gave her spirits a much-needed boost. She climbed another mountain in the Andes alone, reaching 16,000 feet (4923 meters).

The Lima Geographical Society named the north peak of Mount Huascarán "Cumbre Aña Peck" in honor of Annie's climbing achievements.

Two years later she returned to South America to Mount Huascarán. This trip was full of challenges and hardships. The climb was so steep that one of the guides had to cut little steps into the slippery ice to make secure toeholds. Annie was very upset when a special snowsuit borrowed from a museum and a Japanese stove tumbled into a deep crevasse, lost forever. Later, Annie grew alarmed when she realized her left hand had frozen so much it was starting to turn black! She found another layer of clothing to make her warmer and continued with the climb. At last she reached the summit! This victory established Annie as a very important person in mountaineering.

In 1911, at the age of sixty-one, Annie Peck climbed Mount Coropuna in Peru. This was a special climb because Annie carried with her a banner that read, "Votes for Women." As well as a mountaineer, Annie was a suffragette. In fact, she was president of the Joan of Arc Woman Suffrage League. It is not surprising that Annie was an active feminist considering she had worked hard her whole life to follow her dreams and not be inhibited by restrictions placed on women. When she reached the summit of Mount Coropuna, Annie proudly planted this banner. She had high hopes that women who enjoyed mountain climbing in the future would not face the same financial struggles that she had. Earning the right to vote would be one step in the direction toward that equality.

Suffrage is the right to vote; a suffragist is a person who advocates for this right, especially for women, and a suffragette is a woman who advocates suffrage for women.

With her inquisitive nature and love for learning new things, Annie had become quite knowledgeable about South American politics and economics during these expeditions. She was recognized for her expertise in these areas and on more than one occasion was called upon to assist with political disputes.

By the age of seventy-five, Annie was doing less mountain climbing, but her desire for adventure was still strong. She arranged a trip by local airlines around the coast of

South America, stopping in major cities and points of interest along the way. Annie was especially interested in aerial views of the summits of mountains she had climbed. Her wonderful adventure by air took seven months to complete. By the end, Annie was quite exhausted.

The remarkable Annie Peck was a woman full of determination and desire to achieve her goals. She was a university professor, an adventurer, a mountain climber, a writer, an expert on South American politics and economics, a feminist and a resourceful fundraiser. She lived a full life and remained physically active until her last few years. Annie's final climb, at the age of eighty-two, was of Mount Madison, New Hampshire. Before she died in 1935 at the age of eighty-five, Annie managed to fit in one more trip, a relaxing cruise to the West Indies. She had been ill and feeling very weary, but nothing would stop Annie Peck from having this one last adventure!

2

Bobbie Rosenfeld

1903   1969

THE YEAR IS 1922. At the end of a busy day of work at a chocolate factory, a young woman called "Bobbie" hurries to a local women's sports club. She pulls on a pair of baggy black shorts, which she ties at the waist with a thin rope. She tugs an oversized T-shirt over her head, yanks on her running shoes and rushes out to the track. Ahh! This is where she's wanted to be all day. She warms up her muscles, stretches a little and then she's off, tearing around the track. Her breathing is heavy and deep as her long legs race over the pebbly surface. She has a look of fierce deter-mination in her eyes. Fellow athletes at the track smile and wave at her as she whizzes by.

Bobbie Rosenfeld, a Canadian sports legend, was born in Russia in 1903. Her parents named her Fanny, but as an athlete, she was nicknamed "Bobbie." To escape persecution for being Jewish, her family immigrated to Canada when Bobbie was just a baby. She grew up in Barrie, Ontario, winning her first award for athletics at a local track-and-field meet when she was seventeen.

Most athletes are good at just one sport, but Bobbie was a phenomenon, excelling at track-and-field events, tennis, ice hockey, basketball and softball. She was named Canada's Athlete of the Half-Century in 1949 and was admitted to the Sports Hall of Fame by the Canadian Press in 1950. Many people say Bobbie was the most important Canadian athlete of the entire twentieth century!

Standing about 5 feet 5 inches (165 cm) tall, Bobbie didn't look like the powerhouse she proved to be. Friends described her as "wiry" and "quick," but she was also aggressive in her approach to sports. She didn't hold back and because of this was able to achieve great things.

As a teen, Bobbie enjoyed playing softball. At a tourna-ment in Beaverton, Ontario, Bobbie ran so fast that some people organized a small track meet and encouraged her to take part. Bobbie won the 100-yard race. Later, she found out that she had beaten Rosa Grosse, who was Canadian champion at that time! This little race in a small town marked the beginning of Bobbie's remarkable career in athletics.

Bobbie Rosenfeld was named the top Canadian woman sprinter in 1921. Soon after, she moved to Toronto, where there were more opportunities. Here she could train and race with other top athletes. During the weekdays, she worked in a chocolate factory as a stenographer, a person who takes notes in a fast method of writing, called shorthand, and then types them. She ran and played sports in the evenings and on the weekends.

As more young women began working outside the home after the First World War, women's leisure activities changed as well. Women's sports became more and more popular in the 1920s, especially in major cities. One author called this decade "the Golden Age of women's sport in Canada." Women could also now wear baggy shorts and T-shirts while playing sports, rather than long dresses and constricting clothing.

Bobbie didn't just pursue track and field. She played tennis and basketball as well. In fact, in 1924, she won the Toronto grass court tennis championships. She played on many championship basketball teams for Ontario and Eastern Canada.

In 1925, Bobbie was the one and only member of the Patterson Athletic Club's team. The chocolate factory where she worked sponsored the Patterson Athletic Club. It is wonderful that her employer supported her athletic pursuits during a time when many people still thought women had no place in sports. Bobbie competed at the Ontario Ladies' Track and Field Championships and came out shining again. She achieved firsts in the 220 yards, the discus, the long jump, the javelin and the 120-yard hurdles.

For women in sports 1928 was a very significant year. This was the year that women's track and field events were added to the Olympic program. But this didn't happen without lots of controversy. In fact, Canadian doctors attended a special meeting on this topic in Amsterdam, Holland (the Netherlands) — the location of the Olympic Games. While Bobbie and her teammates were busy breaking records and winning medals at the Games, the doctors argued that women should not participate in these "unsuitable" sports! This might seem ridiculous to us considering all the incredible women athletes today, but there were many such obstacles for female athletes to overcome. We owe a lot to the women of Bobbie's generation for showing that women could not only run, jump and score; but they could also break world records, perform spectacularly and stun crowds with their strength, endurance and speed.

Bobbie Rosenfeld set three world records in 1928: one in the running long jump, one in the discus and one in the standing broad jump. Astonishingly, these records were not broken until the 1950s! At the 1928 Summer Olympics, Bobbie was awarded a gold medal in the 4 x 100-meter relay. After the relay, Toronto's *Evening Telegram* reported that the team of four women was "so exuberant that the cameraman, anxious to get their picture, could hardly keep them still." Imagine the excitement! Bobbie also won a silver

Bobbie (right) and her 4 x 100-meter relay teammates in 1928.

medal in the 100-meter race and placed fifth in the 800-meter race. What an experience that must have been for Bobbie Rosenfeld!

There is an interesting story behind Bobbie's slower-than-usual fifth-place finish in the 800-meter race. Bobbie had not trained for this distance and had no desire to win. She competed in this race only to encourage her teammate Jean Thompson to run her very best. When Jean faltered, Bobbie held back and didn't pass her. She coaxed Jean to run faster, letting Jean finish in fourth place, just ahead of her. Such a selfless nature is rarely seen in today's highly competitive world. Bobbie's sporting behavior revealed her strong belief in team spirit and giving others the opportunity to shine in their areas of specialization. She could easily have run her hardest and perhaps added another medal to her collection. But, in this case, Bobbie put her teammate's goals first, setting aside her own competitive nature and assisting Jean to push her hardest and do her best.

Several women collapsed after this 800-meter race. Even though male athletes also collapsed after some events, the women's extreme fatigue was treated as a very serious matter. Women were not allowed to compete in this particular distance again until the Olympics in Rome in 1960. This was a blow to women's athletics, but at least women could still compete in other track-and-field events.

Unfortunately, poor health interrupted Bobbie's athletic career. She suffered from very painful arthritis when she was in her mid-twenties. In 1929, she had to rest in bed for eight months and then she had to use crutches for a full year to get around. Because of Bobbie's strong will and positive outlook she did not feel sorry for herself. She refused to lie in bed for long. As soon as she could, she began playing sports again. She played softball in the summer and hockey in the winter. You would think after suffering such a bout of arthritis she wouldn't compete again but would take it easy. Not Bobbie. She was the best hitter on the leading softball team in 1931. A year later she was appointed top player in Ontario in women's competitive hockey.

In spite of her tremendous success in track and field, Bobbie always said that hockey was her favorite sport. Constance Hennessey of the Toronto Ladies' Athletic Club described Bobbie Rosenfeld as "a fine hockey player ... She checked hard and she had a shot like a bullet ... She was just the complete athlete and I am certain she would have been good at any sport. Certainly, she was as good as one could see in track and field, hockey, basketball and softball."

Bobbie's selfless nature emerged again when she decided to become a coach. In 1932, she joined the Canadian women's track-and-field team as a coach for the British Empire Games, held in London. Her love of track and field and her delight in helping others achieve their goals were very satisfying for her. Unfortunately, the arthritis returned and Bobbie retired from active participation in sports.

She didn't let this obstacle affect her passion for sports, however. With her well-known reputation as a world-class athlete, she used this forced retirement to engage in a new aspect of sports. In 1937, Bobbie accepted a job as sportswriter with a Toronto newspaper, *The Globe and Mail*. Her column was called "Sports Reel." This career was a perfect fit for Bobbie's skills and she worked very hard at her job.

Bobbie Rosenfeld's journalism career lasted for twenty

years. She wrote about all sports: the ones she loved best as well as equestrian events, swimming, cycling and skiing. Her writing showed enthusiasm and nerve, and her sense of humor made her well liked by her colleagues. Bobbie continued to help promote women's sports through her column, which her co-workers described as "outspoken, spirited, candid and humorous." She retired in 1966 due to poor health and died in 1969.

Bobbie's achievements as an athlete, coach and sportswriter would be a cause for celebration today. In her day, they were nothing short of miraculous! Bobbie Rosenfeld is truly one of the greatest Canadian athletes of the twentieth century.

3

Sandra Schmirler

1963   2000

IT IS A CRITICAL POINT in the Calgary curling match between Team Schmirler and Team Kleibrink at the Canadian Olympic trials of November, 1997, for the 1998 Nagano Olympics. Team Schmirler is losing and it looks like Team Kleibrink will go on to represent Canada. A hush falls over the crowd before Team Schmirler's next shot. The four teammates whisper together, conspiring. They have discovered a difficult shot, called a long-angle wick, that could earn them three points — enough to catapult them into the winning position. All the pressure is on Sandra Schmirler as she prepares for the shot. With perfect concentration, Sandra puts all her effort into throwing the stone at the right angle and with the perfect amount of force. In the moments before she performs the shot, she thinks of nothing else. The outside world is a blur. As she releases the stone, Sandra lets out a wild scream of delight. She knows she has made it. Her teammates Marcia and Joan sweep the ice in front of the stone ensuring it will stop in the best position. It does. The crowd explodes with applause.

Sandra Schmirler, world champion curler, grew up in the town of Biggar, Saskatchewan. Sandra's mother and father encouraged their three daughters to always try their best and pursue their dreams. But who would have guessed that Sandra would go on to become an Olympic champion curler affectionately known as "Schmirler the Curler?"

At high school, Sandra was an athletic star. She was good at fastball, volleyball, badminton and swimming. Sandra's true desire was to play hockey, but this wasn't meant to be. It was not common for girls to play hockey in the 1960s and early 1970s and, in any case, Sandra's family didn't have hockey equipment for her. So at age twelve Sandra started curling.

One of Sandra's role models was her grandmother McLeod, who enjoyed curling in her younger years and told Sandra lots of stories about the fun games she had played. Sandra inherited her grandmother's competitive nature. Sandra's other main influence was her father, Art. He used to take Sandra with him when he played pool. Many people agree that there is a similarity between curling and pool: both rely on psychology and strategy.

At her high-school graduation, Sandra won three awards: Sports, Best Overall Student and the Spirit of Youth award. She had also begun curling more seriously and won a provincial high-school title in her last year.

Sandra earned a Bachelor of Arts degree in physical education at the University of Saskatchewan in Saskatoon. She curled on the University of Saskatchewan team for a couple of years. Then she curled on a more competitive team made up of Carol Davis, Heather McMillan and Laurie Secord-Humble. Their first season was terrific, but the second season was less successful. Once she had finished her degree, Sandra moved to Regina where Kathy Fahlman recruited Sandra to become a "third" on her curling team.

It was on this team that Sandra met her best friend and long-time curling teammate, Jan Betker. Jan, like Sandra, was an extraordinary curler. In the 1986–87 season something clicked with the team and they won a number of important bonspiels, or curling matches. At this time, Team Fahlman was made up of Sheila Schneider, Jan Betker, Sandra Schmirler and Kathy Fahlman. The team was pumped to compete at the Scott Tournament of Hearts, a national competition between provincial teams, and hoped to perhaps even get to the Calgary Winter Olympics! At the Olympic trials, Team Fahlman played very well, but placed a disappointing fourth.

> A "third" is the name of a position in curling. It describes the order that the four players throw their curling stones. The first curler is called the "lead," next is the "second," then comes the "third," and last is the "skip." Curling teams are named after the skip.

The following year, Kathy, their skip, was recruited to join another team. At first, Jan and Sandra asked Susan Lang to replace her, but the dynamics weren't quite right and the team didn't do well. Sandra and Jan had a heart-to-heart talk and they decided that Sandra would skip and Jan would be the third, a position she excelled at. Sandra had only played skip at a few fun games and didn't feel very confident about this decision. Amid all these uncertainties, Team Schmirler was born with Marcia Gudereit as lead, Joan McCusker as second, Jan as third and Sandra as skip. Atina Ford played as alternate. Marcia and Joan were soul mates, as were Jan and Sandra. All the women loved playing practical jokes and having fun. Together the foursome made a great team.

On two occasions early in Team Schmirler's existence, Sandra lost her cool. After one critical loss, Sandra stormed out and slammed a door. At another match, Sandra hit a bench with her broom. Marcia and Joan also reacted badly. Sandra and her teammates deeply regretted what they had done. They never acted like this publicly again and always managed to accept losses with sporting behavior.

The 1991 Scott Tournament of Hearts marked a breakthrough for Sandra. Admittedly, it was her second time competing at the Scotts (first with Team Fahlman), but it was an amazing accomplishment for her to be competing at the national level in her first year of skipping! Unfortunately, Sandra was preoccupied with the outcome and intimidated by the other more experienced players. These uneasy feelings affected her concentration and spoiled her game. Luckily, Sandra and her teammates learned another lesson from this experience and kept trying. Later, the team became well known for playing splendidly under extreme pressure.

In 1993, after winning the Scott Tournament of Hearts, Team Schmirler went on to curl as Team Canada and win the world championship crown at the Women's Worlds in Geneva, Switzerland. In 1994, the now-defending champions repeated this win at the Worlds in Obertsdorf, Germany. Disappointment recurred, however, when they lost the 1995 Scott in Calgary and gave up their Team Canada crown. But Team Schmirler was learning to accept disappointments as lessons to keep learning, reminders to focus harder and warnings to never take their winning streaks for granted.

The team's focus shifted back to their families for a while. In 1997, Marcia's first child was just a baby, Joan had her second in the spring and Jan had her first child in the summer. Sandra married Shannon England and became pregnant soon after. Even with their additional family responsibilities, Team Schmirler began competing again. Somehow, the time off seemed to help the team and they returned to the ice with renewed vigor and a thirst for winning.

The reunited team won the 1997 Scott Tournament of Hearts in Vancouver. With three Scott Tournament wins under her belt, Sandra became known adoringly as "the Queen of Hearts." The team solidified its comeback by also winning the 1997 Ford World Women's Curling Championships in Berne, Germany. What an achievement! Finally, after curling — and winning — as Team Canada in 1993, 1994 and 1997, Team Schmirler represented Canada at the 1998 Olympic Games in Nagano. Sandra's superstar team took home a gold medal! Three world championships and one Olympic gold is a truly amazing accomplishment for one team. No other team had ever come close to this level of achievement.

Sandra (right) and her teammates celebrate their gold medal win at the 1998 Winter Olympics in Nagano, Japan

The triumphs of Sandra Schmirler and her team were not only a result of hard work and determination. They were largely a result of the wonderful dynamics of the five women and their coach, Anita Ford. Open discussions and light-hearted joking around ensured that team members hid nothing from one another. Because all of the team members were mothers, they shared many experiences in the challenges of raising babies and young children. Sandra, for example, was breastfeeding her first child at the Olympic trials. All of the curlers juggled motherhood seamlessly with competitive curling. Sometimes they had to take some time off in the later stages of pregnancy but, soon after giving birth, each woman resumed her role on the ice. They always agreed that their families were their first priority in life. Remarkably, they continued to view curling as a hobby even with their stream of fantastic triumphs.

When they encountered challenges in the curling world, remembering their true priorities helped the team overcome the challenges. Their deeply rooted friendships, their Saskatchewan roots, and, of course, their passion for curling and competition all contributed to the winning bond that made Team Schmirler excel. All the women credit the support of their families for giving them the time they needed to focus on their sport.

Chemistry and group dynamics were part of the cement that bound this foursome together. Sandra once said that Joan could make her feel like the best skip in the world! Marcia was quiet and steady on the ice. Joan won points with her pals for always looking on the bright side and boosting their confidence. Jan was renowned for being a fighter who never gave up hope in winning a game — even when the odds were against them. Sandra captured the most media exposure as the skip, but she was remarkably humble and always credited the full team, rather than basking in all the attention she received. Her public profile enabled Sandra to work hard to raise public awareness about women's curling. Her team was respected first not for being female curlers, but for being *excellent* curlers. Maureen Kroll, vice-president of the Edson, Alberta, Curling Club, remarked, "Sandra promoted women in curling, showing that you as a mother and female could have a good showing in the game." The women's different personalities all contributed to the tremendous successes of this team that dominated curling in the 1990s.

Tragically, Sandra Schmirler died of cancer in March 2000, just seven months after being diagnosed with this disease. Her untimely death, at age thirty-six, had a tremendous impact on curlers, athletes and fans through-out the world. Her devastated teammates tried to continue playing, but with little success. The spark that held the team together was gone and with it an era of women's curl-ing genius.

4

Julie Krone

1963

J ULIE KRONE, winner of over 3,500 horse races, including a prestigious Triple Crown race, showed the world that female jockeys could compete and win in top caliber races. In 2000 Julie was the first woman ever to be inducted into the thoroughbred racing hall of fame. Traditionally men dominate horse racing, but Julie didn't let this stand in her way. She became one of the best jockeys in the world.

Growing up on a farm in Eau Claire, Michigan, Julie was surrounded by animals. She had two huge dogs, a cat and a half Arab–half Shetland pony named Filly. Julie first sat on a pony when she was just two years old, and adapted well to her first ride. Her mom, a horse trainer, quickly spotted her daughter's natural talent for riding. Julie learned how to train ponies and feed and water horses when she was still a preschooler.

At the age of five, Julie won first prize at a riding competition for contestants under twenty-one. But she didn't spend all her free time with her pony. Playing tackle football, swimming in ponds and swinging on a tire swing were also part of her childhood. She was aggressive and strong and not afraid of taking risks.

> Liz Hartel from Denmark was the first woman to compete against men in equestrian sports, at the Olympics in 1952. Liz's silver-medal win was even more amazing because she is paralyzed from the knees down. Liz required some assistance to mount and dismount her horse, but once she was seated this amazing athlete put on a spectacular performance!

Julie credits Filly, a strong-willed, sneaky and spirited horse, for much of her early riding success. By riding Filly around her farm as a girl, Julie learned much more than the basics of riding. She learned how to stay on her pony when she bolted. She learned how to adapt her approach when one strategy wasn't working. Once she had mastered riding Filly, Julie was well-equipped to go on and ride other challenging horses. Even after Julie had left home to become a jockey, she fondly remembered her pony, Filly.

After watching eighteen-year-old Steve Cauthen, from England, win the Triple Crown in 1978, fifteen-year-old Julie decided that she was going to become a jockey. Julie practiced racing on a track she made on her farm. She got a summer job at the Churchill Downs racetrack in Louisville (where the Kentucky Derby is held) grooming horses and walking them after races to cool them down. Julie loved the excitement of being at the track. She felt like she was getting a little closer to her dream.

Julie first raced profession- ally in Michigan, Ohio and Illinois in the summer of 1980. She learned a great deal and by July she was starting to win. Julie was so set on becoming a jockey that she decided to leave high school in her last year and move to her grandparents' house in Florida. There, she could take advantage of the warm climate and race year round.

In 1969 Diane Crump was the first woman to ride in a professional race. In the late 1960s Kathy Kusner applied for the license to be a jockey. After much fighting, she managed to secure one, but then never used it.

When Julie first showed up at the racetrack in Tampa to promote herself as a jockey, a woman named Denise, who gave her a lift in her car, mistook her for a child. At 4 feet, 10 ½ inches (1.5 meters) tall, Julie was small and looked young for her age. Denise's trainer, Jerry Pace, took Julie on as an exercise rider and apprentice jockey. In fact, after a mere five days at this track, Julie had her own exercise and jockey's licenses in hand. Jerry boasted, "That girl's going to be a very famous jockey someday, and her picture is going to be on the front of magazines." Jerry had a lot of faith in Julie's future as a jockey. Julie has never forgotten the kindness Jerry showed in giving her that first break.

When she left Tampa to race elsewhere, Julie had trouble finding an agent willing to represent her. (Jockeys need agents to manage their business affairs, arrange which horses they will ride and make bookings for them to race.) Finally an agent in Maryland agreed to take her on. Soon after, Julie had a fantastic offer to ride famous trainer Bud Delp's horses. This was something she had dreamed of but never imagined would happen. She had to change agents to do this, but her first agent was very supportive.

The Triple Crown is a series of three different races. One is the Kentucky Derby, held in Louisville, Kentucky; one is the Preakness Stakes, held in Baltimore, Maryland; and one is the Belmont Stakes, held in New York.

To win a Triple Crown, a horse must win in all three of these races. To do so is a great achievement.

The Triple Crown is the biggest event to win in horseracing.

In 1982, when Julie was nearing graduation from being an apprentice rider to a full-fledged jockey, she was very nervous. An apprenticeship lasts for one year from the date on which the new jockey wins her fifth race. During the apprenticeship period, the horse the apprentice jockey rides is allowed to carry less weight than horses ridden by full-fledged jockeys. This can be a big advantage, so many trainers are willing to take a chance on a new jockey for this reason.

As a "journeyman" jockey, she would no longer have this advantage. (A journeyman is a full-fledged, professional jockey who has completed her apprenticeship.) Julie worried a lot about how she would do after this transition. Her worries dissolved when she won her first four races under her new designation. But bad luck struck in the fall of 1983, when Julie's horse tripped on a loose dressing on one of its legs and Julie tumbled off and broke her back. Her doctor told her to rest for three months. However, after one month, Julie began riding again.

Early in her career as a jockey Julie encountered jealousy and resistance from some other jockeys for being a woman working in a male-dominated sport. Once, a jockey named Miguel Rujano slapped Julie with his whip after losing a race to her. Julie was stunned by the blow, but continued to the scales to be weighed after the race. When she realized her ear was bleeding, Julie could no longer contain her anger. She walked up to Miguel and punched him. After having her picture taken for her win, Julie walked back to the jockey's room. Miguel then threw her into the swimming pool. Julie lashed back by throwing a deck chair at him.

Julie was not proud of this incident with Miguel Rujano. They were both fined and Miguel was suspended for five days. Julie realized that the source of her bad behavior was likely her determination to win, and to prove herself as a female jockey. Later, as Julie became widely known as one of the very best jockeys in the world, she no longer felt the need to act so tough.

Success certainly rained upon Julie Krone. By 1987, she was ranked sixth-leading rider in the United States. She headed to New York, where the winnings were greater and the races of a higher caliber. There, she raced for some of the most celebrated trainers, riding many top thorough-breds. She also rode for less-established trainers and helped them get the lucky break they needed to ensure their own career's future. She met some wonderful people this way and continued to believe that every horse is unique and needs to be handled differently. While riding with the best jockeys in the world, at an international competition in Tokyo, Japan, in 1990, Julie beat her childhood hero, Steve Cauthen.

Julie on her way to the winner's circle.

In June 1993, she won a Triple Crown race at the Belmont Stakes. Julie was the first woman to ever achieve this. This incredible win showered her with publicity. She was interviewed on television and featured on the cover of many popular magazines. Julie won the Women's Sports Foundation Award for Female Athlete of the Year.

On August 30, 1993, Julie had a terrible accident. She shattered the bones in her right ankle and cut her arm badly. Her heart was also bruised when a horse stepped on her chest. Her protective riding vest saved her life. She had three operations in which two metal plates and fourteen screws were used to fix her ankle. Julie couldn't ride for nine months, but she was lucky to be able to ride again at all. This fall was so frightening that Julie had trouble sleeping and lost her confidence. She was suffering from post-traumatic stress disorder, a condition that can be caused by traumas (extremely distressing experiences that cause severe emotional shock). A long period of treatment helped Julie regain her confidence and, once her injuries had fully healed, she began to ride again.

After winning over 3,500 races, riding 15,970 horses and establishing herself as one of best jockeys in the world, Julie Krone retired in April 1999 at the age of thirty-five. This remarkably determined, courageous woman has paved the way for female jockeys in the future.

5

Chantal Petitclerc

1969

"**P**ETITCLERC SHATTERS WORLD RECORD!" "Petitclerc wins second silver!" "Gold ... on track for Canada!"

Headlines boasting Chantal Petitclerc's victories abound. And there is no length of race that she hasn't tried. Chantal set a world record for the 100-meter sprint and holds Canadian records in every length of race. She has competed at the Barcelona (1992), Atlanta (1996) and Sydney (2000) Olympic Games, as well as numerous world championships. Among wheelchair athletes, she placed ninth in the 1997 and 1998 Boston Marathons, and was fifth in 1991. This 1991 race was her best marathon time ever at 1 hour, 59 minutes, 23 seconds. Chantal just keeps making the news with her racing successes.

Chantal Petitclerc was born in Saint-Marc-des-Carrières, a small town in Québec, Canada. French is her first language. As a girl, Chantal wasn't really interested in sports. But when she was a young teen, Chantal was injured in a farm accident when a barn door fell on her. As a result, her legs were paralyzed. Chantal started swimming to stay in shape. She loved the challenges swimming offered her. A few years later, she met wheelchair-racing coach Pierre Pomerleau. Pierre recognized Chantal's determination and thirst for competition and thought that Chantal had great potential as a wheelchair racer. This is how her journey to becoming a champion began.

At eighteen, she tried her first wheelchair race. A friend made Chantal's first racing wheelchair. Her results in this race caught the attention of coaches, sports supporters and fans. She was named "Most Promising Athlete" and won a high-quality racing wheelchair.

Competition wheelchairs are designed differently from regular wheelchairs. They have three wheels: one medium-sized, streamlined wheel straight out front and two large wheels that are angled in toward the seat, which is cut down low. Athletes wear gloves to protect their hands while they turn the wheels.

As a wheelchair racer, Chantal competes in track events. Paralympian track events consist of sprints, relays, middle distance and marathon races. Field events consist of discus, javelin and shot put. Many paralympic athletes compete in swimming events as well. Other summer sports include equestrian events, power-lifting, sailing and table tennis; and team sports, such as wheelchair basketball, rugby and tennis.

Due to the wide variation in physically challenged athletes' physical abilities, there are different classifications for competition depending on the nature of the athlete's disability. For example, quadriplegic athletes, people who have "limited function of both their upper and lower body," are in one competition category, while paraplegic athletics, people who have "minor to no limited function of their upper body," (in other words, the upper body functions well) are in another competition category. Each of the above categories is further subdivided into two categories for track events. Track paraplegics can be either a T3 or a T4 designation. Chantal Petitclerc is in the T4 classification. T4 athletes are more able than T3 athletes.

To prepare for her races, Chantal trains very hard. Her disciplined schedule consists of four hours of training, six days a week. Chantal does weight training and uses a clever device called a roller to train in the winter. A roller looks a little bit like a sled, but works similarly to a stationary bicycle. Chantal takes one month off every year.

Since the summer of 1992, when she was twenty-two years old, Chantal has had many successes in her athletic career. She placed third in both the 100-meter and 800-meter races at the 1992 Barcelona Paralympic Games. In 1995, at the Montreal Marathon and the Kushiro Half-Marathon in Japan, Chantal was first among wheelchair racers. At the 1996 Paralympic Games in Atlanta, Georgia, she placed extremely well, winning five medals overall: gold in the 100- and 200-meter and silver in the 400-meter, 800-meter and 1500-meter races. Chantal set a world record in the 100-meter dash with her time of 16.70 seconds, beating

Australian Louise Sauvage's record by 0.02 seconds.

Chantal won second place in the 800-meter race at the World Championships in Athens in 1997. At the 1998 Worlds in Birmingham, England, she placed first in the 100-meter race and second in both the 800-meter and 1500-meter events. She has had a great string of wins!

The Sydney 2000 Olympic Games were a major high point in Chantal's career. Finally, she beat her almost unbeatable rival Louise Sauvage in the prestigious 800-meter race. Chantal calls this the best race of her life. Unfortunately, there was a dispute about the win. Three other wheelchair racers had collided at the 195-meter point. These three were at the end of the pack of racers. Many argued that they were so far behind Chantal and Louise that they couldn't possibly have beaten either of them. The Canadian Paralympic Committee appealed the decision to cancel Chantal's gold to the International Court of Arbitration. In the end, Chantal kept her gold.

✰ **Did You Know?** ✰

The first Canadian wheelchair race competition was held in Manitoba in 1947.

The first international wheelchair games took place in 1948 in Stoke-Mandeville, northwest of London, England. This small town still holds wheelchair games today.

The first time that wheelchair athletic events were held at the Olympics was in Los Angeles in 1984.

People stopped her on the streets and exclaimed, "Are you the one who beat Louise Sauvage?" Chantal was making history!

Chantal is a vibrant speaker with great presence and

sparkle. She is not shy when giving interviews about her sports career, and has become well liked and recognized. Chantal has also devoted lots of time to speaking on behalf of various associations and charities. She lives in Montréal, Québec — a city with many media opportunities and great connections to the sporting world. Aside from her role in sports, Chantal has used her public-speaking skills in her regular job; she has hosted the television lottery show *Loto-Québec* since 1994. She also hosted the show *Pareil, pas pareil* for two seasons.

On February 9, 2001, Chantal was awarded Female Athlete of the Year by Sports-Québec (Athlètes Excellence du Québec by the Féderation Québécoise d'Athlétisme). Chantal was up against finalists Caroline Brunet (kayaking), Anne Montminy (diving) and Mélanie Turgeon (downhill skiing) for this great honor. In her typically gracious manner, Chantal made a beautiful speech thanking all the people who had encouraged her over the years, including her corporate sponsor. She concluded, "It's been a wonderful adventure and I'd like to share this trophy with all of you."

Do more gold medals lie in store for Chantal Petitclerc? We'll have to wait and see. Chantal is now training for the 2004 Olympics in Athens, Greece. By that time, Chantal will be thirty-four years old. How many athletes have managed to extend their careers over four Olympic Games? Not many! Most athletes are lucky to participate in two Olympics. Chantal has a terrific, never-give-up attitude that has served her well.

✩ 6 ✩

Cathy Freeman

1973

IMAGINE HOW EXCITED you would be to light the huge Olympic Cauldron at the opening ceremonies for the Games. Then, imagine winning a gold medal at those same Games. Think how proud you'd be if this were happening in your own country. This is exactly what happened to Australian runner Cathy Freeman at the Sydney 2000 Olympics.

As a child, Cathy loved to run, and raced with her brother Norm Junior. Her stepfather, Bruce Barber, was impressed by Cathy's finesse on the school track. He decided to coach Cathy himself and bought some books to learn more about coaching. With her stepfather's help, Cathy started to win track meet events at school. Before long, she was hooked!

Cathy Freeman's career as an outstanding athlete began in 1990. She won a gold medal at the Commonwealth Games in Auckland that year, as a member of the winning 4 x 100-meter relay. Cathy was named Young Australian of the Year for her performance in this event.

> After one race that Cathy won by 10 meters, she said "It felt like I stepped up a gear and was flying above the ground."
>
> ✪

Cathy has run in the 100-meter, 200-meter and 400-meter races, and the 4 x 400-meter relay. Her best events are the 400-meter race and the 4 x 400-meter relay. She won first place in both the 200-meter and the 400-meter events at the 1994 Commonwealth Games in Victoria, Canada.

At the 1995 World Championships, Cathy placed fourth in the 400-meter race and was crushed at not achieving the gold medal. She thought she could have done better and was upset with herself.

Cathy bounced back to set a Commonwealth and Australian Record at the 1996 Olympic Games. She won a silver, but her final time in the last heat was a remarkable personal-best time of 48.63 seconds. Cathy's time at this event was 86 one-hundredths of a second slower than the women's 400-meter Olympic-record time of 48.25 seconds, which was achieved by Marie-Jose Perec at the 1996 Olympics. Cathy is more than one second from the world record time for the 400-meter sprint, however. This time was clocked in 1985 at 47.60 seconds and is held by Marita Koch of East Germany. In 1996, Cathy was named Australian Sports Personality of the Year.

After the 1996 Olympics, Cathy told her coaches, "I'll just train harder." This strategy worked well for Cathy. She raced less, but trained harder. This allowed her to perform extremely well in the races that really mattered. At the 1997 World Championships she placed first in the 400-meter race with a time of 49.77 seconds. Australians and Aboriginal people rejoiced with Cathy as she carried both the Australian and the Aboriginal flags around the track for her victory lap. Cathy has always been proud of her Aboriginal roots. In 1998, she was awarded Australian of the Year. She also received the Aboriginal and Torres Strait Islander Sportswoman of the Year Award.

This talented athlete injured her foot in 1998, which forced her to withdraw from the Commonwealth Games. Her determination helped her to get back on the track and build up her strength and speed again. Cathy trained at a resort in Northern Queensland, Australia. Her hard work paid off when she took home a gold for the 400-meter race at the 1999 World Championships. After this, Cathy focused intently on the Sydney Olympics in 2000. Because the Olympics were going to be in her home country, she wanted to excel and make her fellow Australians proud of her. At Sydney, Cathy won a gold medal for the 400-meter race with a time of 49.11 seconds.

"Favorite," "celebrity," "determined" and "champion" are some of the words often used to describe Cathy Freeman. She is also an inspiration and role model to young and indigenous people.

Cathy was honored by Australia when she was asked to

light the Cauldron. This symbolic gesture — lighting the fire to start the Games — was particularly significant because Cathy was representing not only Australians, but also Aboriginal people. Cathy is an active spokesperson for the rights of Aboriginal people.

In fact, Cathy's own family history is what prompted her to get involved with Aboriginal rights. When Cathy's grandmother was just a young child, she was taken away from her family and sent to live with a "white" family. This was part of a government policy of that time to try to make Aboriginal people blend into the general population. These children are now called "the stolen generation." Cathy feels terrible that this happened to her grandmother and sad that she never knew her. However, she is happy that she can now speak out for indigenous people.

Cathy uses the popular image that she has gained through sports to direct the public's attention toward issues facing Aboriginal people in Australia.

Discrimination against Aboriginal people gained much media attention at the Sydney Olympic Games. Cathy Freeman was quoted in newspaper articles published around the world, speaking out for the rights of Aborigines and criticizing the Australian government for its stand on this issue. Now, Australia's human rights record has been questioned by the United Nations.

After her outstanding victory at the Sydney Olympic Games, who knows where Cathy's career will take her? But even when Cathy does retire from racing, she will most likely continue to be a spokesperson for Aboriginal rights. She has earned the respect of all Australians for her athletic achievements and for standing up for what she believes in. Cathy's determination doesn't stop with running. It will carry her far.

7

Chen Lu

1976

WITH FLOWERS IN HER HAIR, costumed in a short, lilac gown, Chen Lu glides smoothly over the ice. She skates to the song "Butterfly" by Mariah Carey and Chen *is* a butterfly, seeming to float as she whirls and jumps in her beautiful routine. Smiling at the finish, her eyes sparkle at the admiring crowd at the 1994 Winter Olympics in

Lillehammer, Norway. Later, when the final results are presented, Chen Lu discovers that she has won a bronze medal! Not only is this a tremendous achievement for Chen, but also she is the first Chinese figure skater to ever do so.

Chen Lu was born in Changchun, the capital city of Jilin province, which is located in the northeast part of China. She first learned to skate when she was four, on a flooded soccer field that was made into a rink. She wore a used pair of boys' skates that were at least a size too big. In spite of this, Chen took very well to this new sport. She seemed to have a natural talent. Because Chen enjoyed both skating and ballet dancing, her father suggested she try figure skating. It was a perfect fit! Chen progressed rapidly.

Before Chen's win, figure skating, a very individualistic sport, was not promoted very much in China. There were no indoor skating rinks and few outdoor rinks. Often Chen would skate very late at night when it was easier to book ice time. Lucky for Chen, her father was the manager of an outdoor rink, so this helped Chen to secure time on the ice.

Chen credits her parents for her

Early in her career, Chen Lu was mistakenly called "Lu Chen," and "Lulu" as a nickname. The mistake was probably caused by confusion over the way people are normally introduced in China (and in other countries, such as Hungary and Japan). In China, Chen Lu would be formally presented as "Lu Chen," with her family name first followed by her personal name. In countries such as Canada and the United States, personal names usually come before family names. Chen Lu has since set the record straight on her name.

Japanese figure skater Midori Ito was the first skater from Asia to ever win a gold medal in figure skating, at the 1989 Worlds in Paris, France. She was also the first woman to successfully land a triple Axel. At the 1991 Worlds, Midori accidentally jumped right out of the skating rink into the camera pit! Seemingly unruffled, she climbed out and continued her routine. Midori was chosen to light the Olympic Cauldron at the opening ceremonies for the 1998 Winter Olympics in Nagano, Japan.

passion for sports. Her father was a member of China's national hockey team and her mother excelled at table tennis — one of the most popular sports in China.

The first coach Chen had, at age four, was a friend of her mother's. When Chen was seven or eight, she switched to Li Minzhu. She stayed with this coach for many years. Chen could do a triple jump when she was only nine years old. No one else in China could do such a difficult move. Chen has tremendous pride and a strong desire to keep trying — two qualities that helped her achieve her goal of perfecting the triple.

Kristi Yamaguchi (American) and Midori Ito (Japanese) are two figure skaters whom Chen looked up to as role models. Like her heroes, Chen Lu possesses incredible poise and grace that have become part of her trademark style. No doubt her many years of ballet lessons also contributed to her delicate approach to difficult skating moves.

In 1990, when she was just fourteen, Chen won the Chinese Nationals and then the World Junior Championships in Budapest, Hungary. She competed very well at the 1992 Winter Olympics in

Albertville, France, placing sixth overall. Later in that same year, Chen placed third at the Worlds in Oakland, California. She repeated this success in the same competition a year later in Prague, Czech Republic [then Czechoslovakia]. (Oksana Baiul from Ukraine was first and Surya Bonaly from France was second.)

Canadian judge Sally Rehorick, impressed by Chen Lu's early competition performances, said, "There's a finish and a polish to her skating for someone so young. She always has programs that use the ice in a surprising way, with unusual angles and ways of approaching jumps."

Chen competed at the 1994 Olympics in Lillehammer, Norway, where she won her bronze medal. China was triumphant! Chen was nationally and internationally recognized for her talents. Unfortunately, shortly after this glory she experienced an injury. Chen was unable to compete at the 1994 Worlds in Chiba, Japan, due to a stress fracture in her foot. This kept Chen off the ice for a full year. But by the time the next World Championships came up in 1995, in Birmingham, Great Britain, she had moved up to number one! This was the first world championship won by a Chinese figure skater.

During the exciting competition at the 1996 World Championships, in Edmonton, Canada, Chen Lu placed second, after Michelle Kwan of the United States. Many fans thought Chen deserved the gold, but this was not the judges' decision. However, Chen earned two perfect 6.0

scores for her wonderful performance.

Then Chen's wave of success flattened. She was crushed with disappointment when she placed twenty-fifth at the 1997 Worlds. This devastating loss didn't make her quit or lose faith in herself, however. Instead, Chen trained with a renewed determination to win. She changed coaches and worked harder than ever. Her self-discipline paid off when she won a bronze medal at the 1998 Olympics. Now Chen had two bronze medals from two different Olympics and numerous great finishes in World Championships as well. She was proud of her accomplishments.

In 1998, at the age of twenty-one, Chen Lu retired from her career as a competitive figure skater. She moved to San Francisco, California, to study. Not wanting to stop skating and performing entirely, the charismatic and skillful Chen skated for new audiences with "Stars on Ice." Then Chen resumed her training and began competing again. The stress fracture in her foot continues to plague her from time to time, but Chen rests when it is painful to allow her injury time to improve. Chen is thrilled to be back on the competitive circuit!

8

Hayley Wickenheiser

1978

"PRACTICE MAKES PERFECT," is one of the sayings Hayley Wickenheiser lives by. She is currently the best female hockey player in the world. Hayley believes that doing drills and training hard are what have made her an outstanding player. Unlike many, she doesn't dread training sessions. Instead, she thrives on practicing shots over and over again until she gets them just right.

Born in Shaunavon, Saskatchewan, Hayley loved being dragged around a skating rink on a sleigh before she could even walk. She was also very interested in watching the National Hockey League on television when she was just a toddler. By the age of four, she was playing hockey for hours on her family's backyard rink. It isn't surprising that by age five, Hayley began playing minor league hockey on a boys' team coached by her father, Tom Wickenheiser. He put her in defence for five years to teach her patience, because she was such an aggressive player. Hayley often had to change in a dark, damp boiler room because there was only one changing room at the rinks. Nevertheless, the boys accepted her as one of the team simply because she was so good. She won "Most Valuable Player" nearly every year. By age ten, her father put her in center and she has never played defence since! When she watched the first women's world hockey championship on television at age eleven, she was terrifically excited. She would not always have to play in a boys' league. Perhaps one day she could be part of a girls' team.

Hayley got her wish after her family moved to Calgary when she was twelve, but was frustrated at first by the less competitive level of play. Four years later, in 1994, she was on Team Canada at the World Championship. This is when things really started to get exciting!

As a member of the women's national hockey team, Hayley helped win four world championships (1994, 1997, 1999, 2000) and a silver medal at the 1998 Winter Olympics in Nagano, Japan. She has played on Canada's national team since 1994, when she was just fifteen years old. Even though she is one of the youngest team members, she is considered to be an experienced player, or a veteran.

Hayley is known as a cooperative team player and an

excellent role model for girls and young women. She has received a great deal of media attention, and has used it to promote women's hockey every chance she gets. In December 2000, Hayley launched a twelve-city, cross-Canada tour, called the Wickenheiser One-On-One Tour. At this development clinic for girls aged ten and up, Hayley encouraged players to keep the puck longer, instead of passing it right away. She says, "In female hockey, players tend to get rid of the puck as soon as possible." Hayley's clinic stressed confidence and finesse on the ice.

Hayley sets aside lots of time for chatting to young athletes and signing autographs. She sees interacting with the public and promoting women's hockey as an important part of her role as a hockey star. Recruiting and encouraging younger players to pursue the sport is essential for the future of women's hockey.

Hayley thinks women's hockey is taking off and that a woman will play in a professional league with men within just five or six years. Does this sound incredible? Maybe not. Hayley now skates with the University of British Columbia's men's hockey team and with injured Canuck players when she is in Vancouver. Already some female players have played on men's amateur teams. Hayley doesn't see this achievement as one of her personal goals, however. She thinks it is more likely that one of the ten-year-olds she talks to today could end up being that special woman who plays on a men's team in five or six years.

There is no doubt that women's hockey is firmly established as a serious sport. In 1998 at the Winter Olympics the Canadian women's team won a silver medal. The female athletes are skilled and play with tremendous spirit and determination. We all know about Wayne Gretzky. His name conjures up images of a hockey genius, a hero and a great professional athlete. Perhaps in a few years the name Hayley Wickenheiser, or that of another female hockey player, will have the same impact on Canadian households. Think of what this will mean to women's hockey — and *all* hockey in Canada!

Hayley has already been paired up with Wayne Gretzky in publicity material for the Canadian Hockey Association. The two were featured on a mailing to 600,000 hockey players and volunteers. It is a sign of progress that women's hockey was not ignored in this national promotion.

Hayley's talent and constant efforts to perfect her hockey skills are not the only ingredients to her success. Hayley is a leader and a team spokesperson. She is tall and strong, which gives her an advantage. She loves competition. She is patient enough not to expect instant results when she is striving for a new goal. Hayley shows intensity and great concentration when she plays hockey. The final motivating factor that drives her to do her best is this: Hayley loves to win!

Remarkably, Hayley doesn't play just hockey very well. She is also an excellent softball player. She began playing softball when she was five years old, and played on the national junior team in 1995. After she was established as a hockey player, Hayley decided to try out for Canada's Olympic softball team. It was one of the biggest challenges of her life, and she was ecstatic when she learned she had made the team. Hayley views herself as a stronger hockey than softball player, because she has spent a lot more time practicing hockey. The coach of Team Canada said it was Hayley's tremendous versatility as a player that landed her a spot on the softball team. Hayley has played in many positions from third base to outfielder and she is a good runner.

After five months away from the ice in 2000, Hayley was anxious to get back to hockey. She skipped her six-week rest period between the 2000 Summer Games in Sydney, Australia, and hockey training, because, like a truly devoted player, she just couldn't keep off the ice. She plans to play hockey for Team Canada again in the 2002 Olympic Games in Salt Lake City. By then, she will be twenty-four, still young for a hockey player.

What does the future hold for this young athlete? Hayley knows that athletic careers are usually short-lived, so she is looking at a completely different type of career when she retires from hockey and softball. Hayley studies science (and plays hockey) at the University of Calgary in the winter, and studies (and plays softball) at Simon Fraser University, Burnaby, British Columbia, in the summer. Her next goal is to enter medical school and become a doctor. There is no doubt that Hayley Wickenheiser sets her goals high!

9

Venus and Serena Williams

**1980
1981**

CURRENTLY RANKED numbers two and four in the world, sisters Venus and Serena Williams are still climbing the professional tennis roster — and the whole world is watching! Venus predicts they will soon be number one in doubles and numbers one and two in singles. "It's reality waiting to happen," she says, with her confident smile.

The Williams sisters began playing tennis before they were five years old. Richard Williams, Venus and Serena's father, coached them while they played on public courts in inner-city Compton, part of Los Angeles, California. Compton was full of gangs, crime and street violence. Describing the concrete courts the girls learned to play on, Richard once said, "We play on two courts — that's all there is — and they look like trash, they're so slippery."

Richard Williams had set up his own security company and phonebook delivery service when they moved to Compton in 1983. He also sold low-cost health insurance to poor people in their community. Having grown up poor in Louisiana, where he was raised by his mother, a cotton picker, college-educated Richard was doing fairly well, though money was still a struggle.

Richard taught himself how to play tennis by studying videos, books and magazines. He had no formal training at private tennis clubs or even at public community centers. After coaching all five of his daughters, he soon recognized that Venus and Serena loved the sport with a passion and were tremendously gifted players. The day he introduced tennis to Venus, he threw over 500 tennis balls to his four-and-a-half-year-old daughter. She hit every one. Soon Richard began calling her "Cinderella of the Ghetto." The Williams trio were a common sight at the public courts in Compton.

In spite of his wish for Venus and Serena to succeed in tennis, Mr. Williams was protective of his daughters. He didn't let them compete for long in the junior circuit because of the stress this would bring them, and so that they could focus on their schoolwork. He constantly reminded them that tennis is just a game. He was put off by the way many parents pushed their children to be more competitive.

Richard's decision to keep Venus and Serena out of the Junior Circuit might be what saved their careers. Many junior players are focused on winning as many matches as possible. While winning is satisfying, it can stand in the way of a player's development. By continuing to practice, Venus and Serena worked on improving their skills. Mr. Williams believed that winning would come about through acquiring excellent tennis-playing skills. The two sisters did just that, and the rest is history! Venus became a professional tennis player as soon as she turned fourteen, which is the minimum age requirement. Serena also went pro when she turned fourteen, about seventeen months after Venus.

Venus and Serena's climb to stardom didn't happen without lots of hard work, however. Both girls were awarded scholarships to attend a Haines City tennis academy for children in Florida. Rick Macci, who ran the school, coached them for six hours a day, six days a week from 1991 to 1995. Since then, their devoted father has continued to coach them as he did in the early days. But the family no longer has to put up with poorly constructed concrete

Did You Know?

Tennis isn't Venus's only strength as an athlete. She is also an excellent sprinter and middle-distance runner.

Venus loves Russian culture and can speak Russian too. She visited Russia during the Ladies' Kremlin Cup tennis tournament in 1997.

In 1998, in Zürich, Switzerland, Venus recorded a record-breaking serve at 127 miles (203 kilometers) per hour. Serena's serve is presently clocked at 119 miles (190 kilometers) per hour.

tennis courts. Now the Williams sisters are in the big leagues!

Venus and Serena try to avoid competing together in the same tournaments by taking turns playing in singles matches. But sometimes they have to face each other on the court. Then, they don't hold back. They play just as hard as they would against any other player, and they certainly don't give the other any advantages just because of their relationship. Venus triumphed over Serena in a singles match at the Australian Open in 1998. Later, she said with a grin, "I'm sorry I had to take you out, Serena." After playing, and losing to Venus, at the 2000 semi-finals at Wimbledon, Serena cried about the loss for more than half an hour. She hadn't played for a few months because she was recovering from injuries. Thankfully, Venus didn't gloat about this win. Serena had lost many points because of her weak forehand, which Venus acknowledged.

Venus and Serena are best friends who love spending time together. Off the court, they are not rivals at all. Venus and Serena live with their parents in Palm Beach, Florida, in the United States. They can play tennis every day in the warm climate of this state.

Their strength and height certainly contribute to Venus and Serena's excellent tennis playing. Venus stands at 6 feet, 1 inch (185 cm) tall, while Serena is also tall at 5 feet, 10 inches (178 cm). Venus can reach farther, but Serena can change direction quickly and is learning to put her muscles to work in packing more punch into her swings. It will be interesting to watch future matches between the sisters!

The Williams sisters have had the kind of impact on the world of tennis that Tiger Woods has had on the golfing world. The traditions of tennis were created by white people,

Black Women in Tennis: Great Players from the Past

Ora Washington, American, 1898-1971

Played with the all-Black American Tennis Association (ATA) in the 1920s and 30s.

Never allowed to play against leading white tennis players due to racist attitudes towards Black people at that time. Retired early in order to give other Black tennis players a chance to win. She was so powerful that she was virtually unbeatable!

Althea Gibson, American, born in 1927

First played tennis in a Harlem neighborhood in New York City. Was soon "discovered" and sponsored by a country club. Won several ATA tournaments. Broke racial boundaries by competing in the U.S. Lawn Tennis Association tournament in 1950. Althea reached the quarter-finals.

In 1957 and 1958, she won the singles and doubles championships at Wimbledon and the U.S. Open at Forest Hills, New York.

Zina Garrison-Jackson, American, born in 1963

Wimbledon Grand Slam finalist in 1990.

Olympic gold medal in 1998.

Grand Slam mixed doubles champion three times!

Active in setting up tennis programs for inner-city youths in Houston, Texas.

---

and built upon the "preppy," whitewashed look and squeaky-clean, classic image popular among the upper classes. Has this affected the Williams sisters? More than you might think. It is rumored that Venus has been called racist names on the court, and was once pushed by another player as she crossed the court. Serena was booed at a California match in March 2001, because Venus had dropped out of the match due to knee problems and the sisters would no longer be competing against each other. In spite of this, the huge numbers of fans who have flocked to tennis tournaments whenever Venus and Serena play prove that these women have many admirers and a lot of support.

Serena, at nineteen, was the 1999 U.S. Open Singles Champion. She was the first of the pair to achieve this pres-tigious win. Her victory occurred while Venus was taking time off, recovering from tendonitis in both wrists. Apparently, Venus was thinking about retiring from tennis. Watching her younger sis-ter win the U.S. Open sparked something in Venus that made her determined to compete again.

Venus returns a shot.

In 2000, at age twenty, Venus made a tremendous comeback. She won the Ladies' Singles Championship at the Wimbledon Lawn Tennis Championships, tri-umphing over the 1999 defending champion, Lindsay Davenport. This victory marked the first time a Black woman had won this title since Althea Gibson in 1957 and 1958. Venus also won the U.S. Open Singles Championship in 2000. Both Venus and Serena held up a trophy after winning the 2000 Ladies' Doubles Championship. They traveled to Sydney, Australia, for the 2000 Olympics and won another gold medal for the women's doubles competition. Venus also won an Olympic gold for her triumph on the courts in the women's singles. The last time a woman won a gold in both events at the same Olympics was in 1924! Later, Venus was awarded *Sports Illustrated*'s "Sportswoman of the Year" title for 2000. It was no wonder Venus achieved this award. She had won thirty-two single matches in a row! Then in August 2001 she won at Wimbledon again. In September of that year, Venus defeated Serena in the final at the U.S. Open to win that title for the second year in a row. That's five Grand Slam titles for the Williams sisters!

> A Grand Slam is a series of four important tournaments, including the Australian Open, the French Open, Wimbledon and the U.S. Open. Each of these four tournaments is sometimes referred to as a "Grand Slam event" or a "Grand Slam tournament," but to truly win the Grand Slam a player must be number one in all four tournaments.
> The last woman to win a Grand Slam was Steffi Graf, of Germany, in 1988.

Both sisters are studying to be fashion designers at the Art Institute of Fort Lauderdale, Florida. They are juggling their studies with their tennis careers. This is why they generally try to keep the number of tournaments they play each year to a minimum. Twelve tournaments is a typical number. Their interest in fashion, combined with their success in tennis and their crowd-pleasing charisma, has attracted the attention of many fashion magazines. The Williams sisters were *Elle* magazine cover girls in January 2001 and they were featured in an article in *Vogue* magazine in March 2001. Never before had an athlete been photographed for the cover image for *Elle*! Venus and Serena just keep breaking new ground.

Venus and Serena's fashion consciousness is just one more way in which they shake the foundations of the traditional tennis world. Tennis outfits are usually white and conform to very conservative tastes. Venus and Serena's tennis garments stray far from this norm. They wear brilliant colors and unique styles that emphasize their individuality. Both sisters earn a great deal of money through contracts with athletic equipment companies.

Venus's Reebok contract is the biggest endorsement deal ever held by a female athlete! This was a monumental moment for women in sports. Many women athletes still struggle to find enough sponsorship to be able to train, buy sports equipment, hire a coach, travel to competitions around the world and compete. They also need enough money to pay their rent and cover their grocery bills like everyone else. Securing their financial future takes away much of the worry that keeps athletes awake at night.

Serena's strong swing.

As part of the Reebok deal, Venus will be launching her own clothing and footwear collection in the summer of 2002. She will have the freedom to try her hand at helping with the design, even though she is still a student. Angel Martinez, executive vice president and chief marketing officer for Reebok, says Venus Williams is "among the most recognizable and exciting young women in the world. She ... is a devoted daughter, sister and role model to inner-city youth and her enormous appeal transcends sports, age, gender, race and geographic boundaries."

In December 2000, both sisters signed a three-year deal with Avon to endorse products. This marks the first time an athlete has ever endorsed a cosmetics company.

One advertisement that featured Venus sports the slogan: "Defy convention." It takes a lot of courage to be female athletes from a minority group in a sport traditionally dominated by white people. The sisters have become role models to inner-city youth, and have been an inspiration to people from all backgrounds. They are skilled at defying convention and causing a stir. Venus may still be slightly more famous, using her powerful personality, her bold presence and her dazzling style — but look out: little sister Serena may not be one step behind for long.

✫ Sources ✫

The stories of the ten amazing athletes came from some of these sources. You can learn more about these women by checking out the books and Web sites yourself.

Annie Smith Peck

Hasday, Judy L. *Extraordinary Women Athletes*. New York: Children's Press, 2000.

Books by Annie Smith Peck that you might find in your local library (and the year they were originally published):
> *A Search for the Apex of America*, 1911.
> *The South American Tour*, 1913.
> *Industrial and Commercial South America*, 1922.
> *Flying Over South America: Twenty Thousand Miles by Air*, 1933.

Web sites:
www.britannica.com
www.xrefer.com
members.aol.com/anniespeck

Bobbie Rosenfeld

Cochrane, Jean, Abby Hoffman and Pat Kincaid. *Women in Canadian Sports*. Toronto: Fitzhenry & Whiteside, 1977.

Ferguson, Bob. *Who's Who in Canadian Sport*, Vol. 3. Ottawa: Sporting Facts Publications, 1999.

Long, Wendy. *Celebrating Excellence: Canadian Women Athletes*. Vancouver: Polestar, 1995.

McDonald, David. *For the Record: Canada's Greatest Women Athletes*. Rexdale, Ontario: John Wiley & Sons, 1981.

Wise, S.F., and Douglas Fisher. *Canada's Sporting Heroes: Their Lives & Times*. Toronto: General Mills Publishing, 1974.

Wolfe, Helen. *A Woman's Agenda 2002*. Toronto: Second Story Press, 2001.

Web site:
www.us-israel.org/jsource/biography/Rosenfeld.html

Sandra Schmirler

Scholz, Guy. *Gold on Ice: The Story of the Sandra Schmirler Curling Team*. Regina, Saskatchewan: Coteau Books, 1999.

Web sites:
cbc.ca/sports
myhero.com/hero.asp?hero=s_schmirler
sportsillustrated.cnn
www.canoe.ca
www.saskcurl.com

Julie Krone

Gutman, Bill. *Julie Krone: Overcoming the Odds*. Princeton, New Jersey: Steck-Vaughn, 1996.

Krone, Julie, with Nancy Ann Richardson. *Riding For My Life*. Boston: Little, Brown, 1995.

McMane, Fred and Catherine Wolf. *Winning Women: Eight Great Athletes and Their Unbeatable Stories*. New York: Bantam Books/Sports Illustrated for Kids, 1995.

Web sites:

www.faldo.atmos.uiuc.edu/BOOKREVIEW/REVIEWS/172
　　　3.html (review of Julie Krone: The Unstoppable Jockey)

horsesetcinc.com/JKFanClub.htm (Welcome to the
　　　Julie Krone Fan Club Homepage!)

sportsillustrated.cnn.com

www.equestrianpages.com

www.horseinfo.com

www.infoplease.com

www.womensblvd.com

Chantal Petitclerc

Web sites:

www.alcan.com

www.athletisme.qc.ca

www.canoe.ca/AthcanAthletes

www.canoe.ca/AthcanDirectory

www.canoe.com

www.chantalpetitclerc.com

www.nlc-bnc.ca

www.townonline.com/marathon/99

Chen Lu

Milton, Steve. *Skate: 100 Years of Figure Skating.* Toronto: Key Porter, 1996.

Milton, Steve. *Super Skaters: World Figure Skating Stars.* Toronto: Key Porter, 1996.

Web sites:
members.nbci.com
news1.thdo.bbc.co.uk
www.bladesonice.com
www.fhy.net
www.geocities.com
www.ontheice.org
www.skate.org
www.southam.com

Cathy Freeman

Web sites:
sports.chickclick.com
www.athletics.org.au
www.athletics.org.au
www.curriculum.edu.au
www.indigenousaustralia.com.au
www.melbournetrackclub.com.au
www.olympics.smh.com.au
www.smh.com.au/atlanta
www.sportsline.com
www.theage.com.au

Hayley Wickenheiser

Etue, Elizabeth and Megan Williams. *On the Edge: Women Making Hockey History*. Toronto: Second Story Press, 1996.
Wilson, Stacy. *The Hockey Book for Girls*. Toronto: Kids Can Press, 2000.

Web sites:
cbc.ca/olympics
www.canoe.ca/HockeyWomen
www.chl.ca/HockeyWomen

Venus and Serena Williams

Web sites:
racerelations.about.com
sportsbusiness.about.com
sportsillustrated.cnn.com
tennis.about.com
www.findarticles.com
www.sikids.com
www.thewilliamssisters.ne
www.time.com/time
www.wimbledon.org

✪ Photo Credits ✪

Cover

Chantal Petitclerc photograph © Jean-François Bérubé. Reproduced with permission.

Serena Williams photograph by Duane Hart, Sporting Image, Australia. Reproduced with permission.

Sandra Schmirler photograph by Mike Ridgewood, courtesy of the Canadian Curling Association.

Hayley Wickenheiser photograph by Dave Sandford, courtesy of the Canadian Hockey Association/ Hockey Hall of Fame.

Annie Smith Peck

All photographs from Shaista Rahman's Web site, members.aol.com/anniespeck.

Bobbie Rosenfeld

All photographs courtesy of Canada's Sports Hall of Fame, Toronto, Ontario, Canada.

Sandra Schmirler

All photographs by Mike Ridgewood, courtesy of the Canadian Curling Association.

Julie Krone

All photographs from the book *Julie Krone: A Winning Jockey,* by Dorothy Callahan (Minneapolis, MI: Dillon Press, 1990).

Chantal Petitclerc

Photograph © Jean-François Bérubé. Reproduced with
permission.

Cathy Freeman

Photograph by Duane Hart, Sporting Image, Australia.
Reproduced with permission.

Chen Lu

Photograph on page 50 by Jim Graves, Ice Sport.
Reproduced with permission.
Photograph on page 53 by Claus Andersen. Reproduced
with permission.

Hayley Wickenheiser

All photographs by Dave Sandford, courtesy of the
Canadian Hockey Association.

Venus and Serena Williams

All photographs by Duane Hart, Sporting Image, Australia.
Reproduced with permission.

All reasonable attempts have been made to locate the
holder of copyright and to obtain permission to
reproduce the photographs included in this book.

AGMV Marquis

MEMBER OF SCABRINI MEDIA

Quebec, Canada
2001